A scene from the 'Life of St Mark', fourteenth century, in Manresa Cathedral, Spain, showing shoemakers with awls, shears for cutting out soft leather uppers, and side-lace ankle shoes.

SHOEMAKING

June Swann

Shire Publications Ltd

CONTENTS

Published in 2003 by Shire Publications Ltd, Cromwell House, Church Street, Princes Risborough, Buckinghamshire HP27 9AA, UK. Copyright © 1986 by June Swann. First published 1986, reprinted 1993, 1997 and 2003. Shire Album 155. ISBN 0 85263 778 0.

Printed in Great Britain by CIT Printing Services Ltd, Press Buildings, Merlins Bridge, Haverfordwest, Pembrokeshire SA61 1XF.

British Library Cataloguing in Publication Data: Swann, June. Shoemaking. — (Shire Album; 155) 1. Footwear industry — Great Britain — History. I. Title. 338.4'768531'00941 HD9787G72. ISBN 0-85263-778-0.

ACKNOWLEDGEMENTS

Much of the material used in this book has been derived from information in Northampton Museum's outstanding boot and shoe collection, probably the largest in the world. It comprises not only footwear, but tools, machinery, pictures, documents, and indeed everything relating to shoes and shoemaking. A major contribution to that collection was made by the late John H. Thornton, former Head of the Boot and Shoe Department, Northampton College of Technology, to whom all shoe students will be forever indebted, and from whose collections much of my material has been taken. Photographs are acknowledged to: the Beaford Archive, Devon, page 30; Victor A. Hatley, Northampton, page 21 (upper); Northamptonshire Libraries, page 18 (upper) and for loan of the negative for page 15 (upper); Northamptonshire Libraries and the British Shoe Corporation Ltd, page 17. I am grateful to the Curator, Northampton Museum, for permission to use all other photographs in this book. The line drawing on page 2 is by Mr D. R. Darton.

COVER: *Oil on panel by David Teniers the Younger: a detail of 'The Shoemaker teaching the linnet to sing' (1640s).*

BELOW: *A Roman riveted shoe (upper, left); a medieval turnshoe (upper, centre); a welted shoe (upper, right); a close tab, welted Oxford shoe (lower).*

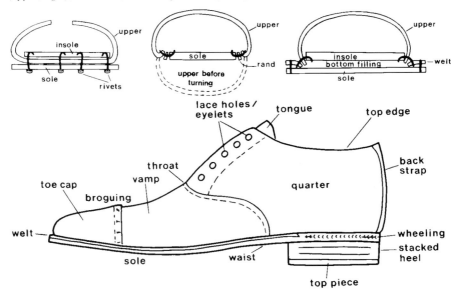

A carving in Rheims Museum, France, of a Roman shoemaker hammering in hobnails, with his kit to hand on the wall and a tub of water for soaking leather under his seat.

FROM ROMAN TO MEDIEVAL

Shoemakers, who have become rare in modern times, should not be confused with cobblers, or shoe repairers. Most shoemakers are capable of doing repairs, but this is usually considered inferior work and left to a different type of craftsman. While the Northampton football team may, perhaps self-mockingly, be called the Cobblers (shoe repairers), shoemakers would be offended if so called.

In early times and small settlements, a shoemaker worked alone, helped by his family. But as towns developed, as they did in Britain in Roman times, shoemakers congregated in streets, usually near the town centre, with more than one worker in each shop. To judge by the 'primitive' societies of the present day, there would be division of labour as soon as two or three people worked together. In the Roman period guilds of shoemakers were formed in Rome, and the fine workmanship found in footwear from Roman Britain suggests that there were guilds here also. Evidence for shoemaking (hammers, knives, awls, offcuts) has been found in towns such as London and Bath and in military forts (a last from Caerwent) and much has come from Hadrian's Wall. Such items have also

3

An altarpiece by the Master of the Carnation, about 1510, from Fribourg, in the Schweizerisches Landesmuseum, Zurich. The top scene shows Saints Crispin and Crispianus in their workshop, one with the moon knife cutting out leather, a bend knife beside him and lasts behind. Below, they are tortured with their own awls.

been found at villas like Lullingstone, and even at small farmsteads.

The Romans, accustomed to a warmer climate, had been used to wearing sandals and in Britain also many surviving leather uppers are cut into straps or exquisitely fine nets, some presumably women's, underlain with contrasting colours and decorated with gilding. As practically no pre-Roman shoes survive, it may be assumed the Romans also brought improved tanning methods. One of the reasons for their conquest was to gain control of Britain's hides.

The construction generally has the edge of the upper (the lasting margin) interleaved between soles and insole, these being thonged together, using a narrow strip of leather round the edge, with a single row up the middle. In addition, the men's footwear and most of the women's and children's were rivetted with a large-headed nail knocked in against an iron last, which turned over the point, forming a rivet. The shoemaker usually sat astride a wooden bench, with the last anvil mounted on it. The hobnails protected the leather on metalled roads.

In the third century two shoemakers Crispin and Crispianus, who according to the French version of the story were born in Rome, were converted to Christianity. During the Diocletian persecutions they escaped to Soissons and supplied shoes and comfort to the poor. The English version says they were born in Canterbury and apprenticed to a shoemaker in Faversham. They were tortured for their faith with their own awls and thrown into the river with millstones round their necks in AD 288. They were first venerated in the middle of the twelfth century, and especially from the fifteenth century onwards. They are usually depicted with one of them standing and cutting out the leather, and the other seated and sewing, typifying the two aspects of shoemakers' work.

In the dark ages invaders brought a totally different culture and lifestyle to Britain. Coming by boat and with no use for Roman roads, they had no need of hobnailed footwear either. It was replaced by the turnshoe in which upper and sole were seamed together inside out and turned, a construction which seems to have originated in the Middle East. It is found in quantities on the Egyptian Coptic sites from the first century AD. The cruder work had been seamed using a leather thong, but this was soon replaced by fine stitching, though the brogue and rivelin makers of Ireland and Scotland continued to use thongs until these were replaced in the nineteenth century by tarred string. The prehistoric moccasin (a rawhide footbag seamed front and back) was revived, especially on the Celtic fringes, but often cut in a complex design rivalling the interlacing in

4

manuscript illustrations. The fineness of the decorative stitching, using a tunnel stitch which penetrates only the surface of the leather, has probably never been surpassed, though no tools have yet been recognised.

Following the Norman conquest, there was a return to stronger materials and, again, possibly a change in tanning methods, as more footwear survives. But as strong leather soles of cattle hide are considerably more common than uppers, the latter were probably of lighter cordwain or cloth. Cordwain leather (originally made from the mouflon, a hair sheep, then from goat and later cattle) was made in Cordoba in southern Spain and imported in great quantities.

The shoes were still of the turnshoe type, usually with a bead welt *(rand)* in the sole seam for greater strength and waterproofing. The uppers were basically a one-piece wrapround, with the seam at the inside waist. With this design, the upper would fit closely only if made of soft material, and it required skill in cutting if the leather was to stretch in the right direction. The first list of shoemaker's kit appears in a shoemaker's testament carol of the last quarter of the fifteenth century: a paring board, tren-chet (knife), lasts, lingels (thread), shoeing horn, turning stick, stirrup, block, bristles, tallow, blacking pot and nails, all recognisable as kit of the 'hand-sewn man' (as makers of handsewn shoes are known) of today.

From the twelfth century, shoemakers began to be found in cities and market towns and near the centres of power, the royal castles. By about 1200, for example, there was a street of cordwainers in the centre of Northampton, and at least one supplied the king and court in the nearby castle. Guilds of cordwainers or shoemakers were formed in Oxford in 1131 and in London before 1160, and most cities and towns followed by the fourteenth century. The Northampton guild was not formed until 1401, when the town had passed its peak as a seat of government, and the regulations became very restrictive in 1452, as the town declined. A unit of measurement of shoe size equal to one third of an inch (a barleycorn) seems to have originated when measurements were standardised in 1305, implying that shoes could now be bought ready-made, as well as bespoke (made to measure). As well as being made for sale in towns, shoes were also sold at the great medieval fairs.

LEFT: *A wooden carving of Saints Crispin and Crispianus, 1534, in the Bally Schuhmuseum, Switzerland. One stands using the moon knife; the other is seated sewing, with his foot on the heel block and a tub of water beside him. There are three other workers behind.*
RIGHT: *Jost Amman's illustration of 'The Shoemaker' in Hans Sachs' 'The Book of Trades', Nuremberg, 1568. Thread and moon knife lie on the bench. The man on the left stitches in the welt, using a double-ended thread.*

ABOVE: *An etching by Adrian van Ostade: 'The Cobbler', 1671, based on his oil of 1657. It shows the poor conditions under which the trade has frequently worked: has the man temporarily ousted the dog from his kennel?*

BELOW: *An engraving by Abraham Bosse: 'The Shoemaker's Shop', about 1633. It is a prosperous shop, with boots, shoes and slippers hung up for sale. The shoemakers all use the stirrup and have baskets of work beside them, while the master, typically, appears to be the clicker, and the mistress winds thread.*

Oil by G. Terborch in Northampton Museum: 'The Shoemaker', 1660s. Using the awl to make a hole for the thread he sews a woman's shoe with a covered wooden heel; his foot on the heel block.

THE SIXTEENTH AND SEVENTEENTH CENTURIES

With the end of the middle ages came a change in construction methods to the *welted shoe*. The upper was henceforth attached to insole and welt, with a second row of stitches through the welt to attach the sole. The hollow made by the addition of the welt was filled with a cork mixture, which, together with the flexibility of the welted shoe, made it probably the most comfortable shoe devised. The other change in construction was the moving of the principal upper seam to the centre back, producing the traditional vamp and pair of quarters. Though perhaps the least sensible position for a seam, it persists to the present day.

With the decline of Britain's main industry, wool, in the sixteenth century towns specialising in other trades began to emerge. The apprentice books for Northampton, for instance, show that by the 1580s the weavers and woolcombers were taking fewer apprentices and were replaced by shoemakers and cordwainers as the dominant trade. It appears that the medieval restriction of three apprentices still survived, but there were two firms, the Gutteridges and the Pendletons, who took the maximum allowed, each apprentice being quickly replaced by another when 'out of his time'. These were obviously sizable firms, which today we would call manufacturers.

They probably resembled the London firm of Simon Eyre, as portrayed in Thomas Dekker's play *The Shoemakers'*

Holiday, written in 1599. Eyre, the master shoemaker, employs at least three journeymen (one of whom is referred to as the foreman) and a boy. They seem to live on the premises. Eyre rises to become Lord Mayor, after typically making his fortune when his ship comes home, for there never was much profit in shoemaking. It has always been highly skilled and labour-intensive, and shoemakers, with their intimate knowledge of human foibles, have likewise always been soft-hearted. It was in the 1580s that the trade was first referred to as the 'gentle craft', and much is made of it in the play.

It seems likely that Dekker and Thomas Deloney, whose book *The Gentle Craft* had been published two years earlier, were reflecting this new importance of the shoe trade. One of the characters, a nephew of the Earl of Lincoln, does not scruple to pose as a shoemaker to court his lady, and Eyre himself claims 'the gentle trade is a living for a man through Europe, through the world'.

The play also confirms what can still be seen today amongst makers of handsewn shoes: when two or three work together, there is division of labour, with each man doing one operation on a pile of ten or twelve shoes, before passing them on to the next. For the journeymen make a pair of shoes for Ralph's wife before he goes off to the war: 'cut out by Hodge [the foreman – this being the operation requiring the greatest skill, if the leather is not to be spoilt and wasted], stitched by my fellow Firk, seamed by myself.'

There is also lively satirical comment on the current fashions, when Eyre's wife becomes Lady Margery and asks the men to make her a pair of shoes: 'cork, good Roger, wooden heel too' – a reference to the introduction of heels, which were just coming into fashion. Heels created a problem for shoemakers, because of the extra quantity of lasts then required to allow for different heel heights. This was solved by making lasts and shoes 'straight', that is, to fit either foot, like socks, not shaped for right and left, a practice which continued for the next two hundred years, until improvements in the pantograph in the early nineteenth century made it practical to produce mirror-image pairs of lasts again.

Oil on panel by Jan Miel in Northampton Museum: 'The Itinerant Cobbler', about 1630. He carries a roll of leather and a few tools on his back, making a precarious living if all his customers were as poor as this.

By the time of the Civil War in the 1640s the modern pattern of shoemaking had begun to emerge. Orders for army boots and shoes were given to groups of shoemakers in London (twenty shoemakers are mentioned in connection with the New Model Army in 1645) and in Northampton, where thirteen shoemakers, led by Thomas Pendleton, gained a contract for six hundred pairs of boots and four thousand pairs of shoes for the army going to Ireland in 1642. However, although they fulfilled other contracts and were satisfactorily paid, in 1651 they were still complaining that the first bill had not been paid and, as far as it is possible to ascertain, there seems to be £208 still owing: this is typical of shoemaking, though perhaps the buyers felt justified in refusing to pay for the troop of horse hired to ensure the shoes reached the right destination in London.

Northampton had shown itself capable of supplying army boots on a large scale, and this it has continued to do to the present day. The town has specialised in men's wear: different skills and ability are required for women's work, and close contact with high society and fashion leaders is essential, if the shoemakers are to keep up with fashion. London, as the capital, has always been able to do this, and the women's trade has concentrated

8

there, although other regional centres have succeeded too: Oxford in the seventeenth century, York and Bristol, depending on what resorts were fashionable.

This growth swamped the old medieval guild system, and although Northampton adopted a constitution for the trade in 1656, this was the last one before the combinations and manufacturers' associations in the nineteenth century. In towns such as Carlisle and Edinburgh, where the industry was smaller, the guilds grew again in the eighteenth century, celebrating St Crispin's Day with banners and processions, and they merged imperceptibly with modern practice during the Napoleonic Wars.

FROM THE EIGHTEENTH CENTURY TO 1856

In 1725 Daniel Defoe in *The Complete English Tradesman* described the dress of Englishmen, and he wrote of their shoes that they were 'from Northampton for all: the poorest countryman and the master', but he did not mention women's shoes. So Northampton had gained its reputation and continued to expand through the eighteenth century, supplying with its cheaper labour shoes for the London market and for export to the growing empire. Shoemakers' advertisements in the local newspaper in 1764 listed the styles made, with their price

bespoke and a cheaper price for ready-mades, though these had been widely available by 1725. In the 1740s sale shoes became common enough for shoemakers to think it worthwhile to put their names in them, and printed labels with name and address appear stuck on the sock.

Shoes were no longer sold only in the shoemakers' own shops and by haberdashers, but by 1746 there were establishments described as country shoe warehouses, stocking shoes from a variety of sources, and these became common by the 1780s. In towns most shoes were

Women's buckle shoes by John Came of Cheapside, London, about 1750, in Northampton Museum. One of the few shoemakers to make a fortune, he bequeathed it to charity.

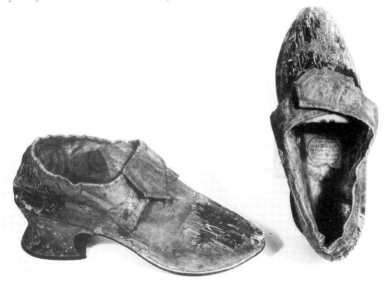

ABOVE: *A coloured etching published by J. Evans: "New Boots and Shoes', 1797. There are few fittings in the shop, while the shoemaker's knee serves as footstool. The gentleman tries on boots, using the straps, his discarded shoes with their separate buckles in the foreground.*

BELOW: *A coloured mezzotint by an unknown artist: 'Cobler's Hall', about 1778. In a rather grand living room, the shoemaker works by the window, birdcage overhead, and his wife cooks dinner on the fire behind. Shoemakers have been noted for keeping birds since at least the middle ages.*

An etching by Henry Liverseege: 'The Village Politician', 1829. Shoemakers were literate before most craftsmen and were noted for their strong interest in politics.

made by outworkers working at home; some manufacturers employed a considerable number and collected their products into a warehouse. The 1764 edition of *Low Life* painted a vivid picture of workers paid on a Saturday night in 'the Yorkshire and other country shoe houses in almost every public street in London'. Stafford's staple trade changed in the later eighteenth century to shoemaking, with the help of its native-born member of parliament, Richard Sheridan, and impetus was given to the Norwich industry at the end of the eighteenth century by the Napoleonic wars.

In London by the 1730s the market had grown so much that small master shoemakers (only the kit and half a crown were required, it was said) were setting up workshops wherever they could, often in wholly unsuitable garrets. Robert Bloomfield, the poet, left Suffolk as a boy of fourteen to join his brother in one of them: 'It is customary in such houses as are let to poor people in London to have light garrets fit for mechanics to work in. In the garret where we had two turn-up beds and five of us worked, I received little Robert. As we were all single men, lodgers at a shilling per week each, our

beds were coarse, and all things far from being clean and snug, like what Robert had left at Sapiston. Robert was our man to fetch all things to hand. At noon he fetcht our dinners from the cook's shop; and any one of our fellow workmen that wanted to have anything fetcht in, would send him, and assist in his work and teach him, for a recompense for his trouble. Every day when the boy from the public house came for the pewter pots, and to hear what porter was wanted, he always brought the yesterday's newspaper. The reading of the paper we had been used to take by turns; but after Robert came, he mostly read for us...because his time was of least value.'

Because of conditions like these and the huge demand for army boots, the London men had formed trade combinations before 1806 and were threatening strikes. For the first and only time, shoemakers appear as less pleasant characters than the traditional gentle craft. The market was filled with yet more boots from Northampton. Its manufacturers formed an association and opened a warehouse in Smithfield in 1812. Ladies took up shoemaking, in place of needlework, and M. I. Brunel began to rethink how to make boots using unskilled

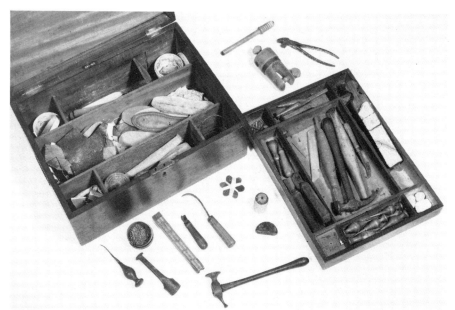

ABOVE: *A set of lady shoemaker's tools of 1803 in the Museum of Leathercraft. It was fashionable from then to about 1820 for ladies to make their own shoes in place of needlework. Additions to the kit were made later.*

BELOW: *A sketch by John Leach for 'Punch', 1854: a father with three daughters being fitted by the shoemaker with new stout boots in their own home.*

labour, mainly wounded soldiers. In 1810 he patented his sole-rivetting machine. Rivetted soles had not been used in Britain since Roman times, and as this was a period of classical revival it is possible that Brunel had seen Roman shoes. As with the Romans, a nail was knocked in against iron, now an iron-plated last. Brunel also designed a press for cutting out the leather. But part of his factory burned down after the war ended in 1815, the need for army boots had ceased, and the rigid rivetted boot was out of tune with the post-war mood. So their manufacture was temporarily abandoned, though not forgotten, and it

ABOVE: *A coloured engraving by Isaac Cruikshank: 'Shoeing Asses', 1807. It satirises the wartime fashion of the dandies for wearing boots with iron 'horseshoes' on the heel. Patent leather and a high polish were also fashionable.*

RIGHT: *Anonymous print: 'Training boys in an Institution', about 1850. The poor orphans look none too happy in their work. They are using clamps to hold the uppers during sewing.*

seems likely that the press continued in use. In 1853 Thomas Crick of Leicester patented his method of rivetting boots, and with the outbreak of the Crimean War the next year he had more success, for machines were devised in the 1860s and rivetted footwear was made in huge quantities up to the First World War.

In the 1770s, after the British colonies in North America had been lost in the War of Independence, they quickly suffered a shortage of shoes and skilled shoemakers. Although France partly filled the market, it too was looking for new methods to bypass the long years of training to make a proficient shoemaker.

ABOVE: *Ladies' boots from the Great Exhibition, 1851. The elastic-side boot shows the welt before the sole is stitched on, and was made by J. Sparkes Hall of Regent Street, London, the inventor in 1837 of elastic sides.*

LEFT: *Northampton Museum's 'Cobbler's Shop', with four venerable shoemakers, when it was set up in 1913.*

Anonymous print: 'The Northampton Shoemaker', 1866. Working at home with his wife sewing the uppers, the shoemaker attaches the sole, with the inevitable advice from an onlooker.

The first textbook on shoemaking, de Garsault's *L'Art du Cordonnier*, appeared in France in 1767 and John Rees's *Art and Mystery of a Cordwainer* in London in 1813. Both describe sophisticated constructions not easily learnt, while outworkers' samples show a perfection of fine stitching (as one might expect when Beau Brummell ruled fashion), a skill acquired after long years of practice. The American solution was to use a wooden peg instead of an iron rivet, and this also gave better wear in wet conditions. Pegs had been used in making heels since their introduction in the 1590s, and in quick repairs to the sole. In 1833 Samuel Preston patented his pegging machine, which was gradually improved, and the method gained ground in Britain in the late 1840s. Mass production of footwear began in Lynn, Massachusetts, just north of Boston, from where they were exported, and this was to bode ill for the British industry.

France was defeated in the Napoleonic Wars and turned to manufacturing with renewed vigour. By the late 1820s huge quantities of French shoes were flooding the British (and American) markets, creating labour problems in Northampton. Its petition to the House of Commons in 1829 spoke of the distress in the industry 'owing to the want of regular employment and the low price of wages'. The imports were chiefly women's wear from Paris, still the fashion leader: narrow black or white flimsy satin shoes survive by the hundred, marked *gauche* or *droit*, and frequently bearing the maker's label, such as Melnotte, who had shops in London and Paris. Attempts to stem the flood by imposing a tax on imports had no effect, even London makers, such as Marsh of Oxford Street, advertising French shoes, though it began to be rumoured that the 'French' shoes were being made in the small workshops of the East End of London, and 'French' boots in Northampton, thus eventually solving the problem. With the growth of the empire, Britain too increased its exports, with sons and cousins setting up warehouses in the cities of Canada, Australia and South Africa.

A Singer closing machine in Northampton Museum, for sewing the parts of the upper together. It was introduced in 1856-7, though the last patent date on it is 1854.

15

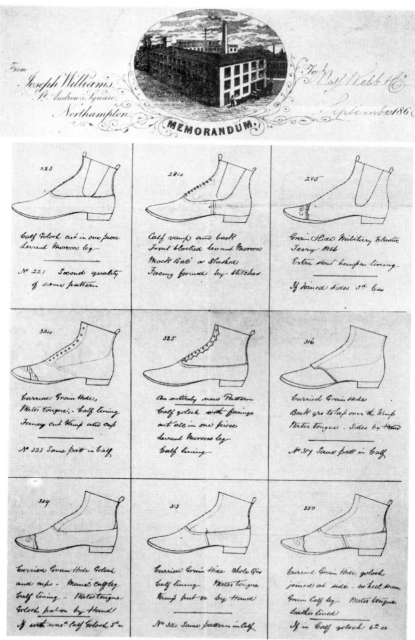

Illustrated letterhead (top) from Joseph Williams, upper manufacturer, Northampton, 1866, with drawings (below) showing some of the range of elastic sides and lace boots offered. Some of the work is still 'by hand'.

"*Any 'casion for a laster?*"

The outwork department of Manfields about 1890. Workers' samples were known as occasioning shoes.

FROM 1856 TO 1914

The Crimean War, like many wars before and since, marked a turning point for the shoe industry. The Singer sewing machine had been introduced from America (as were nearly all shoe innovations in the nineteenth century). Originally for sewing cloth, in 1856 it was modified to stitch leather. A small treadle machine was tried out in Bostock's shoe factory in Stafford. Though quickly abandoned because of resistance from the workers, who had seen machines revolutionise manufacture in other industries during the previous ninety years, it was tried in Northampton, London and other places in 1857. In the same year the first recognisable factories were built in Northampton, one by Isaac, Campbell and Company of London, with Moses Manfield next door. They were of three storeys with semi-basement, a design copied by most subsequent town factor-

ies. Built on the highest part of the old town, they towered over the shoemakers' two-storey houses (Manfield's even had a higher bell-tower in Victorian Venetian style) and, combined with the fear of machines, they promptly caused a strike. Manfield, an astute but honest man, who had walked from Somerset with only his kit on his back thirteen years before, assured the workers it was only a warehouse and the floor had to be reinforced a few years later when heavier machines were invented.

The first machine was merely for closing the uppers, which had traditionally been women's work, frequently done by the shoemaker's wife (easily understandable for women's shoes, which had fabric uppers from the seventeenth century onwards). Although the shoemakers claimed their skills could never be replaced by machines, inventors proceeded

A machine closers' factory, Northampton, from 'Good Words', 1st November 1869. The women seated on the left are sewing (closing) the uppers with treadle machines. The girls tie knots at the ends of seams. The women on the right are fitters and appear to be hammering the seams flat.

to mechanise each hand operation to produce the same welted shoes, rather than to rethink how to make shoes with machinery, as Brunel had done earlier.

Besides the press for cutting out leather, a blocking machine for shaping boot fronts was introduced early. The American Lyman Blake had perfected his machine for stitching on soles by about 1864. Like the early sewing machines, this used a chain stitch, but it is a very sturdy machine, 5 feet 6 inches (1.68m) high, and some are still in use. Although the treadle Singers, bought on hire purchase, could be used by outworkers, the Blake machine was too big and expensive

to have at home and required power to drive it. It was this machine which demanded factories and drove the workers into them. It was turned by overhead belting, the power for which usually came from steam engines.

In the 1860s, too, rivetting and pegging machines, improved during the American Civil War, were adopted in Britain, and factories to accommodate them were built very quickly in all the shoemaking areas. The growth of the trade in Leicester dates from this period. Gradually, over the next thirty to thirty-five years, the various hand processes were mechanised, and the makers of handsewn

Clicking by hand at the Kettering Boot and Shoe Protective Society Limited in 1910. Hand clicking survives today for fine work and samples.

18

shoes, who had operated in most towns, were squeezed out of business, as they could not invest in the machines. One firm which was able to make the transition, through the enterprise of the proprietors, was Clarks of Street in Somerset, where there was little alternative employment. They had begun as sheepskin slipper manufacturers, and the Rossendale Valley too began slipper manufacture (carpet slippers this time), turning to cheap shoes from the 1880s onwards.

In 1874 the National Union of Boot and Shoe Rivetters and Finishers was formed, to cope with this enormous change. At first it involved only the rivetters, the first to be affected on a large scale by mechanisation, and the

The Blake sewer, 5 feet 6 inches (1.68 m) high, for sewing on soles, 1890s, in Northampton Museum. Originally treadle-operated or driven by overhead belting, this example has been converted to electricity. This is the machine which forced the workers into the factories.

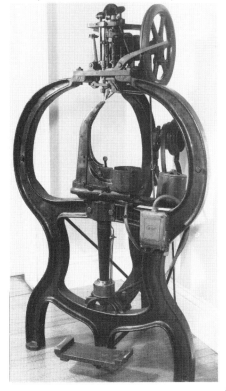

A pulling-over machine in the factory of J. Sears and Company, Northampton, between 1903 and 1913. It replaced the lasting pincers (shown top right in the photograph of the lady's kit on page 12).

finishers, who were determined their job would not be mechanised. The finishing processes became increasingly complex in the last quarter of the nineteenth century, and an ever greater range of tools was required to postpone mechanisation. Finishing was the last process to be fully mechanised, and the end product was so beautiful that people kept the bottoms of their shoes as highly polished as the tops.

But mechanisation was not the only problem. America's expansion westwards had produced enormous enterprise and wealth, space to spread factories using a more efficient single-storey system and, uninhibited by tradition, new ideas for machines. By the 1880s Britain was feeling the effect of what became known as the 'American invasion', of huge quanti-

19

ABOVE: *The village shoemaker at Little Houghton, near Northampton, late nineteenth century. With arms outstretched pulling through the thread, he stitches in the welt. Most village shoemakers had become repairers by the First World War and went out of business between the wars.*

BELOW: *Thomas Amos of Long Buckby, Northamptonshire, aged seventy-four, sewing long boots at the end of the nineteenth century. The village specialised in them, and the trade survived to the end of the twentieth century.*

Brick-built shops (that is workshops), at the end of gardens in Long Buckby, 1964. Built early in the twentieth century, some are still used.

Frederick Cook's Castle Factory, Long Buckby. Eleven men making long boots, about 1900.

Sandy Walker and Henry Larner hand-finishing army boots at Earls Barton, Northamptonshire, soon after 1902. The boots were sent from Rushden 10 miles (16 km) away, and this was the last out-finishing.

FACTORY RULES

This Factory is open to Unionists and Non-Unionists **without distinction.** Coercion or interference of any kind between Workmen is not permitted. Any breach of this **Rule** must be immediately reported to the Firm.

The Posting up of any Notices except with the sanction of the Employer is forbidden. Shop Meetings must not be held in any part of the Premises, nor collection of money made for any purpose whatever, except with the permission of the Firm.

1. From the 1st Monday in April to the Saturday before the 1st Monday in October, inclusive, this Factory will be opened at 7.30 a.m., and close on
at   p.m., on
at   p.m., and on Saturdays at   p.m.

2. The doors will be locked for half an hour after opening time, then opened to let in late comers, after which they will continue locked for the remainder of the morning or afternoon, as the case may be.

3. No interval is allowed to Day Workers for Lunch, but for Tea they may suspend work at   o'clock for   minutes. (The time allowed for Tea forms no part of the 54 working hours.) Piece Workers who require Lunch are to commence same at 10.15 during Summer hours, and at 10.30 during Winter hours, and not to take longer than 15 minutes. Tea same time as Day Workers.

4. When the Factory is opened at 7.30 a.m Dinner Hour is from 12.30 to 1.30, and when it is opened at 8 a.m., Dinner Hour is from 1 to 2.

5. Operatives are to confine themselves to their own department of the Factory, and no one will be admitted to any part of the Factory except the actual employees. Any other person is to apply first at the Office or Counting House, and should any person or persons not in actual employ of the Firm be found on the premises without permission, he or they will be required to leave forthwith.

6. Operatives are required to proceed quietly with their work, and to complete same with reasonable despatch. Any Piece Worker leaving work undone for more than 24 hours will be liable to have such work taken away. The hours for shopping work are as follows :—
Lasters
Finishers

7. Should a Piece Worker be kept waiting for work more than an hour, he may request permission from the Foreman to leave the Factory, and may not re-enter except at the times before specified.

8. All Operatives on weekly wages are required to give, and they will receive, one full week's notice to leave, to expire on the ordinary pay day except in cases where the Manufacturer and Operatives have mutually agreed to waive the practice of giving and taking notice.

9. Operatives are strictly forbidden to take any of their Employer's goods or any work, whether made or unmade, off the premises without permission, or any parcel without a pass from the foreman of his department. Should any man desire to raise any question as to the quality of work, or to claim any extra, he is to follow the Arbitration Rules strictly.

10. Swearing, using obscene language, singing, shouting, or unnecessary noise; sending out for beer or other intoxicating drink; throwing leather or other articles at each other, and writing or drawing upon the walls or doors of the Factory, are forbidden.

11. Smoking is strictly forbidden in any part of the premises, and no light may be struck until the smoker is clear of the Factory.

12. Operatives are expected :—
  1. To be as economical with the Gas as possible.
  2. To keep each man to his own peg where pegs are provided.
  3. To flush w.c's after using.

13. From the 1st Monday in October to the Saturday before the 1st Monday in April, both inclusive, the times of opening and closing above specified will, in every case, be half-an-hour later.

BY ORDER OF THE NORTHAMPTON MANUFACTURERS' ASSOCIATION.

The strict factory rules drawn up by Northampton Manufacturers' Association in the 1890s. Note the long hours (fifty-four per week).

ties of imports, from cheap mass produced poor-quality footwear to highly desirable fashion boots and shoes. The United States was beginning to take a leading place in the world. Shoemakers went to study their methods. Manfield built a new, single-storey factory, with an imposing two-storey office frontage, on the edge of Northampton in 1892, and

again led the field. He also began retailing in his own shops, in the principal cities of Britain and Europe, where the quality of his products was highly appreciated.

In the 1880s there were strikes, which resulted in a standard working week of fifty-four hours, and restrictions on boy labour, so that there was more work for

ABOVE: *The silk banner of the Northampton Branch of the National Union of Boot and Shoe Operatives, with a painting of St Crispin and the various shoe processes, about 1910.*
BELOW: *Pocock Brothers Stores, possibly in Brighton, November 1909. The firm was established in 1815 and was then a manufacturer. Prices range from 1s 3d for children's shoes to 10s 9d, almost a week's wages, for men's calf boots. The crowded display is typical.*

the men. There were further strikes through the early 1890s, until in 1894 the union demanded that no more work should be done outside. In 1895 came 'the last strike', the great lock-out when the manufacturers were determined to crush the agitators. The settlement was a brilliant piece of work truly worthy of the intelligent men who had always been present in the industry, literate when most trades were not, and with their understanding of the weaknesses of human nature. The settlement has survived, chiefly because every two years wages are re-negotiated and linked with the cost of living.

The only major labour problem followed in May 1905 when the Raunds army bootmakers marched to London to protest against the system of tendering,

ABOVE: *Frederick Cook's South Place Works, Long Buckby, built in 1903 as a progressive single-storey factory, photographed in 1909. It was noted for high-class riding boots.*
BELOW LEFT: *A girl's boot from the set made for arbitration purposes after the 1887 Northampton strike, precipitated by the American invasion. It is inscribed with the date, the quality and the signatures of the President of the Manufacturers' Association and the Union representative.*
BELOW, RIGHT: *Pages from Barratt's 'Boots by Post' catalogue, 1916. Their shoes were fashionable, well made and always good value, and they supplied the medium ranges.*

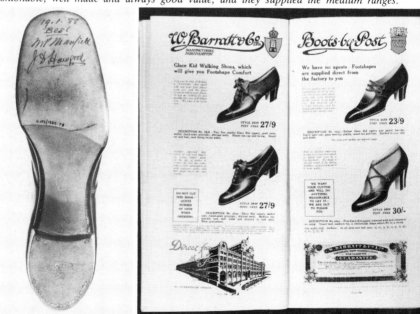

which kept their wages so low. This was the first protest march. The weather was fine and town bands came out to meet them. They held a rally in Trafalgar Square, as so many have done since, and some men recalled it as the most memorable week in their lives, though tendering for army contracts is still a precarious business.

With the labour troubles solved, and with the setting up of the British United Shoe Machinery Company in 1899, which leases machinery to manufacturers, the industry was as efficient as America's. The 'invasion' was brought under control by 1913, when an article in *The Economist* for 13th May was entitled 'Victory for British Boots', and the war next year finally decided the matter.

ABOVE: *The packing department, Kettering Union Boot and Shoe Protective Society Limited, 1910, with the plain boxes used before their advertising potential was developed. The racks were used to wheel the boots round the factory.*

BELOW: *The new Footshape Works built in 1913 for W. Barratt and Company Limited, established in 1903. The first manufacturer to advertise boots by post, in 1903 (workmen's boots at 9s 9d), their advertising campaign from 1935 onwards, 'Walk the Barratt Way', made Northampton's name known all over the world.*

ABOVE: *The making room at the Wellingborough Boot and Shoe Manufacturing Company Limited in 1916. Russian Cossack boots are being made and a high proportion of the workers are young boys.*

BELOW: *The rough stuff department at the Mounts Factory Company, Northampton, in 1919. Heels are being cut and made in the foreground, with a revolution press on the left, and there are still more than the usual number of women hands.*

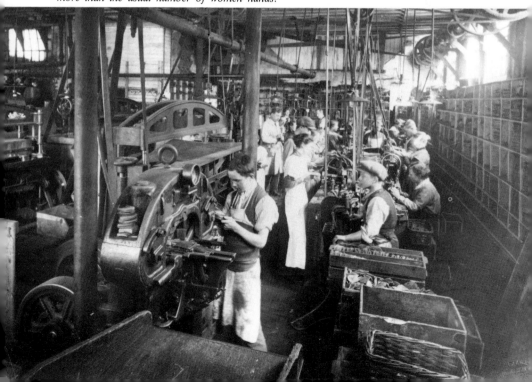

Army boot repairers from Long Buckby in the 4th Northamptonshire Regiment, working in the field, 1917.

FROM THE FIRST WORLD WAR
TO THE PRESENT DAY

The First World War brought disruption of working practices on a scale probably never seen in Britain before. Able-bodied shoemakers volunteered and were drafted into the forces, their places in the factories being taken by women. About seventy million pairs of footwear were produced for the forces of Britain and its allies, over two thirds of them in Northamptonshire. The making of Russian Cossack boots there, at the time of the 1917 revolution, has passed into folk memory. *The Shoe and Leather News Biographic Directory,* written towards the end of the war and published in 1919, reveals the trade's contribution, describing firm after firm together with the sons of the proprietors or directors serving with the forces or killed in action.

Another trend can be seen there too. For many of the sons were training for the professions, as lawyers or doctors, and not following their fathers, the founders of the firms, into the trade. Those with wealth and ability were ceasing to manufacture. The family firms were becoming limited companies run by boards of directors, and this trend continued through the 1920s. With the uncertainty of trade then, Northamptonshire turned, from having made mainly men's wear for two to three hundred years, to

the women's fashion trade and produced some very attractive shoes. Manfield's shoes, light and elegant, sold well, even in Paris and Brussels.

But the 1929 slump confirmed the trade's fears. Many factories went on short time, the usual practice in the shoe trade (since outwork, no doubt), rather than close completely. Indeed, some claimed not to have worked a full week between the two world wars. Wages were correspondingly low, but the standard of craftsmanship had probably never been so consistently high. Apart from the Rossendale Valley products, shoes were built to last and were good value when money was in short supply. A high proportion of production continued to go for export, but from about 1935 the enterprise of Bata in Czechoslovakia saw cheap shoes coming from Eastern Europe.

The pressures also produced an innovation for women's fashion shoes, having the sole cemented on, a process first patented in Barcelona in 1932. This direct vulcanising was exploited in Britain from 1949 by Clarks of Street. The process of change had been accelerated by the development of new adhesives in the Second World War, when again the skills of the shoemaker were in demand, making for the British forces and their allies, including the United States. Some Northamptonshire firms which made shoes for American soldiers have done well in exporting products of similar quality since the war ended.

After the war and the following years of austerity, the trade began to change again in the 1950s. The first direct moulding machine was introduced in 1950. This moulded the sole on to the upper, a method which was to become common by the end of the decade, as changes in style made the end product more acceptable. The army changed to direct moulded soles in 1961. Paris was declining as

LEFT: *Using the grader for varying sizes, Mounts Factory Company, 1919. Brassbound patterns hang on the wall.*

BELOW: *The closing room at the Mounts Factory Company. Stitching the upper sections together had traditionally been women's work, because of the lighter nature of the materials, and this has continued since mechanisation.*

The making room, Mounts Factory Company 1919; crowded and noisy, with the overhead belting.

A London last works in the 1930s. One man does the traditional handworking, while another operates the massive BUSMC last-turning machine on the left.

The Hood Rubber Company's cut soles department at Shoreditch, London, about 1910, showing the typical cubby-holes and baskets used from when they were established in 1885. From 1903 they controlled the British and European business of Hood, Massachusetts, making shoes and rubber wellingtons.

fashion leader, and by the early 1960s Italian shoemakers, with their small flexible companies, able to change fashion quickly, were beginning to send exports to Britain and influence styling. The development of plastics and synthetic leathers continued until they became viable for shoemaking about the same time, all requiring new skills. By the late 1960s huge new machines had been developed, virtually taking plastic in one end and turning out plastic 'bag' shoes at the other, no more desirable on the foot than on the head. The new materials have brought a revolution in shoemaking, as big a change as from turnshoe to welted shoe in 1490. By 1967 leather-soled footwear constituted only 9 per cent of that worn, while 99.5 per cent of women's soles were non-leather. In the 1980s there was a reaction to the plastics, especially since rising oil prices made leather more competitive again.

In 1953 Charles Clore, a property millionaire, bought the shops of Sears (True-Form), in prime high street positions, and acquired with them the factories in Northampton. From then until 1962 he bought other shoemakers, forming the British Shoe Corporation, whose policy was to keep the shops profitable. The Corporation led the way in importing fashionable but cheap shoes, especially from the third world, and transferred its headquarters to a new warehouse in Leicester in 1966. The many factories were rationalised and, with the new materials, workers felt they had become mere assemblers of components and copiers of Italian styling. By 1985 two-thirds of shoes in the shops were imports, since 2000 90 per cent, in spite of continual pressure for import controls. Over 50 per cent of the world's shoes are now made in China, 74 per cent in Asia in general. In Britain shoemakers of quality with enterprise are surviving, but labour costs are not competitive. While one questions whether it is sensible to lose the ability to design footwear to wear in different parts of the world, it is not practical to send to the Far East for Service boots, which for over 350 years have habitually revived the British industry. The lesson of Lynn, Massachusetts, needs to be learnt. In the 1890s it had terrified every British shoe manufacturer; it was reduced a century later to one working factory, and that for children's shoes. Can Britain afford to lose the expertise built up over centuries?

Delivering repairs in Devon about 1930. Country workshops disappeared as the shoemakers retired and the business ceased to attract the next generation.

FURTHER READING

Baynes, Ken and Kate (editors). *The Shoe Show, British Shoes since 1790*. Crafts Council, 1979.

Bordoli, E. *The Boot and Shoe Maker* (four volumes). Gresham Publishing Company, 1935.

Brooker, Keith. 'The Northampton shoemakers' re-action to industrialisation'. *Northamptonshire Past and Present*, volume VI, number 3, pages 151-9. 1980.

Clarke, Jane (editor). *Manual of Shoemaking*. Various editions from 1966.

Clarks of Street, 1825–1950. C. & J. Clark, 1950.

C. & J. Clark, 1825–1975. C. & J. Clark, 1975.

Devlin, James. *The Guide to Trade, the Shoemaker* (two volumes). London, 1839, 1840.

Fox, Alan. *History of the National Union of Boot and Shoe Operatives, 1874–1957*. Blackwell, 1958.

Garsault, M. de. *L'Art du Cordonnier*. Paris, 1767.

George, M. Dorothy. *London Life in the Eighteenth Century*. Penguin, 1966. (See especially pages 196-202.)

Goubitz, Olaf; van Driel-Murray, Carol; and Groenman-van Waateringe, Willy. *Stepping through Time, Archaeological Footwear from Prehistoric Times until 1800*. Netherlands, 2001.

Harrison, Martin. 'The development of boot and shoe manufacturing in Stafford, 1850–1880'. *Journal of the Staffordshire Industrial Archaeology Society*, number 10, 1981.

Hatley, Victor A., and Rajczonek, Joseph. *Shoemakers in Northamptonshire, 1762–1911. A Statistical Survey*. Northampton Historical Series number 6. Victor A. Hatley, 1971.

Leno, J. B. *The Art of Boot and Shoe Making*. The Technical Press, 1949 (identical to 1895 edition).

Mander, C. H. Waterland. *History of the Guild of Cordwainers*. London, 1931.

McDowell, Colin. *Shoes, Fashion and Fantasy*. Thames & Hudson, 1989.

The Modern Boot and Shoe Maker (four volumes). Gresham Publishing Company, 1917.

Mounfield, P. R. *The Footwear Industry of the East Midlands*. University of Nottingham, 1967.

Mounfield, P. R.; Unwin, D. J.; and Guy, K. *Processes of Change in the Footwear Industry of the East Midlands*. University of Leicester, 1982. (Covers the period from 1957.)

Muscott, Bruce. 'Boots and shoes'. *Victoria County History for Northamptonshire*, volume II, 1906.

Northampton Museum. *Shoe and Leather Bibliography*. 1983.

The Patron Saints of Shoemakers. Bally Schuhmuseum, 1965.

Plucknett, F. *Boot and Shoe Manufacture*. London, 1931.

Rees, John F. *The Art and Mystery of a Cordwainer*. London, 1813.

Saguto, D. A. 'The "mysterie" of a cordwainer'. *Chronicle of the Early American Industries Association*, volume 34, number 1, March 1981. (On eighteenth-century shoemaking.)

Salaman, R. A. *Dictionary of Leather-Working Tools*. Allen & Unwin, 1986.

Swann, June. *Shoes*. Batsford, 1982. (Shoe styles from 1600 to 1980.)

Swann, June. 'Mass production of shoes'. *Journal of the International Association of Costume*, number 14, pages 41-53. Tokyo, 1997.

Swann, June. *History of Footwear in Norway, Sweden and Finland*. Kungl Vitterkets Historie och Antikvitets Akademien, Stockholm, 2001.

Swaysland, E. J. C. *Boot and Shoe Design and Manufacture*. Tebbutt, 1905.

Thornton, J. H. *Textbook of Footwear Materials*. National Trade Press, 1955.

Thornton, J. H. 'Left-right-left'. *Journal of the British Boot and Shoe Institution*, volume 7, number 4, August 1956.

Thornton, J. H. 'The iron seamstress'. *Shoe and Leather Record*, 19th November 1959.

Thornton, J. H. 'J. Martin of Taunton on the art of cordwaining, 1745'. *Journal of the British Boot and Shoe Institution*, November 1968, pages 260-1.

Thornton, J. H. 'Brunel the bootmaker'. *Journal of the British Boot and Shoe Institution*, August, September and October 1969.

Thornton, J. H. *Textbook of Footwear Manufacture*. Butterworth, 1970.

Thornton, J. H.; Swann, J. M.; Swallow, A. W.; and Rector, W. K. 'Excavated shoes to 1600'. *Museum Assistants Group Transactions* 12, 1973.

Wright, Thomas. *The Romance of the Shoe*. Farncombe, 1922.

PLACES TO VISIT

Museum displays may be altered and readers are advised to telephone before visiting to check that relevant items are on show, as well as to find out the opening times.

GREAT BRITAIN
Clark's Shoe Museum, 40 High Street, Street, Somerset BA16 0YA. Telephone: 01458 842169. Website: www.somerset.gov.uk/museums

Manor House Museum, Sheep Street, Kettering, Northamptonshire NN16 0AN. Telephone: 01536 534219. Website: www.kettering.gov.uk

Norfolk County Museums, Shirehall, Market Avenue, Norwich NR1 3JQ. Telephone: 01603 493625. Website: www.museums.norfolk.gov.uk (Ask if the shoemaking displays are on show.)

Northampton Central Museum, Guildhall Road, Northampton NN1 1DP. Telephone: 01604 838548. Website: www.northampton.gov.uk (The largest collection of shoes and shoemaking material in the world.)

Snibston Discovery Park, Ashby Road, Coalville, Leicestershire LE67 3LN. Telephone: 01530 278444. Website: www.leics.gov.uk/museums/snibston

BELGIUM
National Schoeiselmuseum, Wijngaardstraat 9, 8700 Izegem. Telephone: 0032 (0) 51 26 87 40.

CANADA
Bata Shoe Museum, 327 Bloor Street West, Toronto M5S 1W7. Telephone: 001 416 979 7799. Website: www.batashoemuseum.ca

CHINA
China Shoe Museum, PO Box 081-926, 200081 Shanghai.

CZECH REPUBLIC
Obuvnicke Muzeum Svit, Tomase Bati 1970, 762 57 Zlin.

FRANCE
Musée de la Chaussure, Ancien Couvent de la Visitation, 2 Rue St Marie, 26100 Romans-sur-Izère, Drôme.

GERMANY
Deutsches Leder- und Schuh-museum, Frankfurterstrasse, D-63067 Offenbach. Telephone 0049 (0) 69829 7980. Website: www.ledermuseum.de

Schuhmuseum, 19 Dinkelbachstrasse, Pirmasens, 678.

Schuhmuseum (Sports), Adidas, Herzogenaurach.

Stadt Museum, Schloss, 485 Weissenfels.

ITALY
Civice Museo della Calzatura, Palazzo Crespi, Vigevano PV.

Museo Salvatore Ferragamo, Palazzo Spini Feroni, Via dei Tornabuoni 2, 50123 Firenze.

JAPAN
Japan Footwear Museum, Matsunaga, Fukuyama, Hiroshima.

MEXICO
'El Borcegui' Shoe Museum, Calle Bolivar, 26, Col. Centro, CP 060000 Mexico.

NETHERLANDS
Nederlands Schoenen & Lederwaren Museum, Elzenweg 25, 5144 MB Waalwijk. Website: www.schoenenmuseum.nl

SPAIN
Museo del Calzado Antiguo, Casa de S. Felipe Neri, Gutat Vella, Barri Gotic, 08002, Barcelona.

SWITZERLAND
Bally Schuhmuseum, Villa Felsgarten, Oltnerstrasse 6, CH 5012, Schönenwerd.

UNITED STATES OF AMERICA
Center for the History of Foot Care and Foot Wear, Temple University School of Podiatric Medicine and the Foot and Ankle Institute, 8th at Race Street, Philadelphia, PA 19107-2496. Website: www.podiatry.temple.edu

Lynn Heritage Center, 590 Washington Street, Lynn, Massachusetts. Website: www.state.ma.us